W9-ARS-328

Major US Historical Wars

WORLD WAR I

John Ziff

Mason Crest
Philadelphia

Mason Crest
450 Parkway Drive, Suite D
Broomall, PA 19008
www.masoncrest.com

© 2016 by Mason Crest, an imprint of National Highlights, Inc.
All rights reserved. No part of this publication may be reproduced or transmitted in any form or by any means, electronic or mechanical, including photocopying, record- ing, taping, or any information storage and retrieval system, without permission from the publisher.

Printed and bound in the United States of America.
CPSIA Compliance Information: Batch #MUW2015.
For further information, contact Mason Crest at 1-866-MCP-Book.

3 5 7 9 8 6 4 2
Library of Congress Cataloging-in-Publication Data

     ISBN: 978-1-4222-3362-7 (hc)
     ISBN: 978-1-4222-8602-9 (ebook)

Major US Historical Wars series ISBN: 978-1-4222-3352-8

Picture Credits: Everett Historical: 7, 15, 17 (left), 19, 21, 32, 40, 51; Library of Congress: 9, 13, 24; National Archives: 27, 28, 30, 34, 39, 48, 50, 54; National Guard Heritage Collection: 1, 43; © OTTN Publishing: 11; Photos.com: 47; US Military Academy at West Point: 17 (right), 37, 49.

About the Author: Writer and editor John Ziff lives near Philadelphia.

TABLE OF CONTENTS

KEY ICONS TO LOOK FOR:

Text-dependent questions: These questions send the reader back to the text for more careful attention to the evidence presented there.

Words to understand: These words with their easy-to-understand definitions will increase the reader's understanding of the text, while building vocabulary skills.

Series glossary of key terms: This back-of-the book glossary contains terminology used throughout this series. Words found here increase the reader's ability to read and comprehend higher-level books and articles in this field.

Research projects: Readers are pointed toward areas of further inquiry connected to each chapter. Suggestions are provided for projects that encourage deeper research and analysis.

Sidebars: This boxed material within the main text allows readers to build knowledge, gain insights, explore possibilities, and broaden their perspectives by weaving together additional information to provide realistic and holistic perspectives.

Introduction

by Series Consultant Jason Musteen

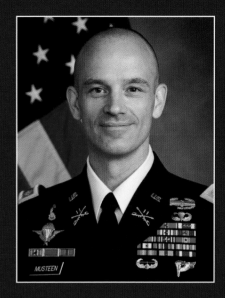

Lt. Col. Jason R. Musteen is a U.S. Army Cavalry officer and combat veteran who has held various command and staff jobs in Infantry and Cavalry units. He holds a PhD in Napoleonic History from Florida State University and currently serves as Chief of the Division of Military History at the U.S. Military Academy at West Point. He has appeared frequently on the History Channel.

Why should middle and high school students read about and study American wars? Does doing so promote militarism or instill misguided patriotism? The United States of America was born at war, and the nation has spent the majority of its existence at war. Our wars have demonstrated both the best and worst of who we are. They have freed millions from oppression and slavery, but they have also been a vehicle for fear, racism, and imperialism. Warfare has shaped the geography of our nation, informed our laws, and it even inspired our national anthem. It has united us and it has divided us.

Valley Forge, the *USS Constitution*, Gettysburg, Wounded Knee, Belleau Wood, Normandy, Midway, Inchon, the A Shau Valley, and Fallujah are all a part of who we are as a nation. Therefore, the study of America at war does not necessarily make students or educators militaristic; rather, it makes them thorough and responsible. To ignore warfare, which has been such a significant part of our history, would not only leave our education incomplete, it would also be negligent.

For those who wish to avoid warfare, or to at least limit its horrors, understanding conflict is a worthwhile, and even necessary, pursuit. The American author John Steinbeck once said, "all war is a symptom of man's failure as a thinking animal." If Steinbeck is right, then we must think.

And we must think about war. We must study war with all its attendant horrors and miseries. We must study the heroes and the villains. We must study the root causes of our wars, how we chose to fight them, and what has been achieved or lost through them. The study of America at war is an essential component of being an educated American.

Still, there is something compelling in our military history that makes the study not only necessary, but enjoyable, as well. The desperation that drove Washington's soldiers across the Delaware River at the end of 1776 intensifies an exciting story of American success against all odds. The sailors and Marines who planted the American flag on the rocky peak of Mount Suribachi on Iwo Jima still speak to us of courage and sacrifice. The commitment that led American airmen to the relief of West Berlin in the Cold War inspires us to the service of others. The stories of these men and women are exciting, and they matter. We should study them. Moreover, for all the suffering it brings, war has at times served noble purposes for the United States. Americans can find common pride in the chronicle of the Continental Army's few victories and many defeats in the struggle for independence. We can accept that despite inflicting deep national wounds and lingering division, our Civil War yielded admirable results in the abolition of slavery and eventual national unity. We can celebrate American resolve and character as the nation rallied behind a common cause to free the world from tyranny in World War II. We can do all that without necessarily promoting war.

In this series of books, Mason Crest Publishers offers students a foundation for the study of American wars. Building on the expertise of a team of accomplished authors, the series explores the causes, conduct, and consequences of America's wars. It also presents educators with the means to take their students to a deeper understanding of the material through additional research and project ideas. I commend it to all students and to those who educate them to become responsible, informed Americans.

Chapter 1

PRELUDE TO A CATASTROPHE

"**Y**ou will be home before the leaves have fallen from the trees." That's what *Kaiser* Wilhelm II told German troops marching off to war in early August 1914.

Like their emperor, most Germans thought the conflict that was beginning would be brief. And soldiers and civilians alike joyously welcomed the fight. "We none of us got to sleep till three o'clock in the morning, we

French soldiers on their way to the front lines take a break in August 1914. When the conflict began, both sides believed that it would end quickly. No one envisioned that the First World War would result in more than 15 million dead and would completely redraw the map of the world's nation-states.

WORDS TO UNDERSTAND IN THIS CHAPTER

front—a line of battle or zone of conflict between armies.

Great Powers—the most important states of Europe in the period leading up to World War I.

Kaiser—a German emperor in the period 1871–1918.

nationalism—loyalty to one's own ethnic group or people, which is often expressed as a demand for an independent state.

neutrality—the state of not aiding or supporting either side in a conflict.

ultimatum—a demand or set of demands issued by one state to another, the rejection of which is considered a cause for further action such as war.

were so full of excitement, fury, and enthusiasm," a 23-year-old recruit wrote of the day his barracks learned that war had been declared. "It is a joy to go to the *Front* with such comrades. We are bound to be victorious!" Throngs of cheering civilians lined the train tracks as the young recruit and his unit moved out.

Germans were hardly alone in the enthusiasm with which they greeted the outbreak of hostilities. In Vienna, the capital of Austria, an observer found "parades in the street, flags, ribbons, and music burst[ing] forth everywhere." Multitudes of hat-waving men, and women blowing kisses and throwing flowers, gave French soldiers a giddy sendoff in Paris. Vast crowds assembled outside the Winter Palace in St. Petersburg and sang Russia's national anthem. Vast crowds assembled outside Buckingham Palace in London and sang "God Save the King."

Europeans from all classes and backgrounds were swept up in a tide of patriotism. Few questioned what their leaders said about the looming war. Most people assumed their country would prevail quickly—if not before the autumn leaves had fallen, then at least by Christmas.

Rivalries and Alliances

Just a few months earlier, an all-out war in Europe had seemed almost unthinkable. None of the continent's *Great Powers*— Britain (or, more formally, the United Kingdom), Germany, France, Austria-Hungary, and Russia—had fought against another for more than 40 years. Europe enjoyed rising prosperity. That prosperity was driven largely by a growth in cross-border trade and investment.

Beneath its placid surface, though, Europe contained dangerous currents. The Great

In the early years of the twentieth century, Germany's ruler Kaiser Wilhelm II began to strengthen Germany's military. Particularly concerning to the British government was the Kaiser's expansion of the Imperial German Navy, which made it one of the most powerful fleets in the world and a potential threat to Great Britain's vast overseas empire.

Powers were engaged in a massive military buildup. Between 1890 and 1913, military spending increased more than 150 percent in both Austria-Hungary and Germany, more than 115 percent in Britain, and more than 90 percent in France.

Europe's military buildup underscored a sobering reality. The continent's Great Powers may not have fought one another for a long time. But their rivalries ran deep. Kaiser Wilhelm, for example, resented the fact that Germany had few overseas colonies, whereas the British and French empires were vast. The Kaiser made it clear that he intended to change that situation. And colonial issues were just one source of friction in

Europe. Distrust among the Great Powers was rampant. To some degree, all of them felt threatened.

To protect themselves against possible aggression, the Great Powers formed military alliances. Germany and Austria-Hungary, along with Italy, entered into the Triple Alliance. The pact committed each of its members to fight in support of any other member that had been attacked by two countries.

A military alliance between France and Russia was intended mostly to deter German aggression. But it bound the two partners to come to the other's aid in the event of a threat from any member of the Triple Alliance.

Britain was something of a wild card in Europe's system of alliances. From the 1860s on, it had avoided becoming entangled directly in continental affairs. Under the foreign policy dubbed "splendid isolation," Britain focused on administering its worldwide empire. But the Kaiser's imperial ambitions eventually prompted a shift in British policy.

In 1904, Britain signed the Entente Cordiale ("friendly understanding") with France. It wasn't a formal alliance. It simply resolved some diplomatic issues between the two countries, which were longtime adversaries. In the wake of the agreement, however, British and French military officers began consultations. From those discussions emerged an informal (and secret) understanding: Britain would help France in a conflict if British interests were also threatened.

Three years after the Entente Cordiale, Britain signed an agreement with another longtime rival. The Anglo-Russian Convention settled colonial disputes in Asia.

The 1904 and 1907 pacts led to the formation of the Triple Entente, an alliance between Britain, France, and Russia. It served as a counterweight to the Triple Alliance of Germany, Austria-Hungary, and Italy. However, the Triple Entente wasn't formalized by a treaty. Britain had no legal obligation to support France or Russia militarily, regardless of the circumstances.

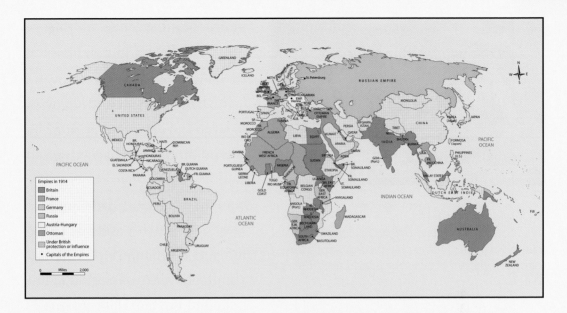

In 1914, European countries dominated the globe. The British Empire alone covered about one-quarter of earth's land area. Germany's desire to expand its own empire was a major cause of World War I.

Because of the rival alliances, a conflict between two of Europe's Great Powers could easily touch off a huge, catastrophic war. Many people assumed their leaders would be extremely reluctant to take that risk. Such optimism was misplaced. "All sides are preparing for European War, which all sides expect sooner or later," wrote Helmuth von Moltke, head of Germany's General Staff, in December 1912. A year and a half later, an assassination would set in motion a chain of events that led to the war Moltke anticipated.

An Assassination in Sarajevo

On June 28, 1914, Archduke Franz Ferdinand—heir to the Austro-Hungarian throne—was shot to death. His wife, Sophie, was also killed. The murders took place in Sarajevo, capital of Austria-Hungary's troubled province of Bosnia-Herzegovina. Authorities arrested the shooter and a handful of others who had plotted with him to kill the archduke. They were all from Bosnia-Herzegovina. But an investigation quickly found that the

Archduke Franz Ferdinand is pictured with his wife, Sophie, moments before his assassination in Sarajevo. The killing on June 28, 1914, caused an international crisis that would lead Europe to war.

plotters had received help from military officers in neighboring Serbia.

Austrian officials had long considered the Kingdom of Serbia a mortal threat. Serbia was a small country, but Serbian leaders were bent on expanding their borders. They believed any area with a significant ethnic Serb population should be part of Serbia. That included Bosnia-Herzegovina.

But the Serbs were only one of a handful of Slavic peoples in Austria-Hungary. In all, Slavs made up nearly half of Austrian emperor Franz Josef's approximately 50 million subjects. Austrian officials worried that Serbian successes might inspire broader Slavic *nationalism*. And that could tear Austria-Hungary apart.

The assassination of Franz Ferdinand presented Austria with an opportunity to punish Serbia. But there was a problem: Serbia enjoyed close relations with Russia. Russia had been stirring up Slavic nationalism on the Balkan Peninsula, where Serbia and Bosnia-Herzegovina were located. It was unclear how Russia would react if Austria attacked Serbia.

Before going to war with Serbia, Austrian officials wanted a guarantee of German support in the event Russia came to the aid of Serbia. Kaiser Wilhelm secretly gave such a guarantee on July 5.

War!

On July 23, Austria-Hungary presented Serbia with an *ultimatum*, or set of demands. Serbia was given 48 hours to accept the ultimatum in its entirety. Failure to do so, it was understood, would result in war.

Austro-Hungarian officials had deliberately made the terms of the ultimatum humiliating for Serbia. They wanted to ensure Serbia rejected the ultimatum. That way, they could say the Serbians were responsible for the coming war. To their surprise, though, Serbia accepted nearly all of the demands, and it signaled a willingness to work out what minor differences remained. Nevertheless, Austria-Hungary cut off diplomatic relations immediately after receiving Serbia's response to the ultimatum.

Kaiser Wilhelm thought Serbia's acceptance of almost all of Austria-Hungary's demands meant that "every cause for war has vanished." Wilhelm decided to personally broker a peace deal. It would begin with Serbia agreeing to let Austro-Hungarian troops occupy Belgrade, the Serbian capital.

On the morning of July 28, the Kaiser directed Foreign Minister Gottlieb von Jagow to inform Austria-Hungary of his plan, and to instruct Germany's ally not to declare war. But Jagow didn't deliver Wilhelm's message. He was, in fact, working behind the scenes to get Austria-Hungary to go to war immediately.

Many historians believe that, by late July 1914, Germany's military leaders had secretly decided to use the dispute between Austria-Hungary and Serbia to precipitate a wider European war. Moltke and his colleagues were convinced that Germany would eventually have to fight a war against Russia. Although Russia in 1914 was much less developed than Germany, it was industrializing rapidly. So the sooner a war was fought, the better Germany's chances of winning.

In any event, on the evening of July 28, Austria-Hungary declared war on Serbia. Two days later, Russia's emperor, Tsar Nicholas II, issued a mobilization order. That meant the country's reserve soldiers were to report to designated centers for possible military duty.

Late at night on July 31, Germany demanded that Russia cancel its mobilization within 12 hours. Russia didn't heed the ultimatum. On August 1, Germany declared war on Russia. That same day, France began mobilizing.

On August 3, Germany claimed that French forces had bombed the German city of Nuremberg. That was a lie, but it served as the pretext for Germany's declaration of war on France.

Britain was pulled into the burgeoning conflict when Germany invaded Belgium. An 1839 treaty obligated Britain to guarantee Belgium's *neutrality*. On August 4, as the Kaiser's troops poured across the Belgian border, the British declared war on Germany.

Austria-Hungary declared war on Russia on August 6. Six days later, France and Great Britain declared war on Austria-Hungary.

The lines were now drawn. Germany and Austria-Hungary (known as the Central Powers) faced off against the Allies (France, Russia, and Britain). World War I—dubbed the Great War by the generation that fought it—had begun.

 # TEXT-DEPENDENT QUESTIONS

1. Name the countries that formed the Triple Alliance. Name the countries that formed the Triple Entente.

2. What happened in Sarajevo on June 28, 1914?

3. Which German action pulled the British into the war?

 # RESEARCH PROJECT

Choose one of the following countries: Austria-Hungary, Germany, Serbia, Russia, France, or Britain. Using the Internet or a library, research what the country's political and military leaders said and did in the month after the assassination of Franz Ferdinand. What, if anything, might they have done differently to avert the war? Present your findings in an essay, making sure to cite evidence to support your conclusions.

Chapter 2

CRUEL DISILLUSIONS

ermany had one powerful enemy, Russia, on its eastern border. It had another, France, on its western border. Mounting a full-scale offensive on both fronts at the same time would be impossible. Germany simply couldn't muster enough troops.

Belgian soldiers wait for a German attack near Namur, on the Meuse River. German war plans had counted on quick passage through Belgium, but the unexpected Belgian defense in August 1914 disrupted the Schlieffen Plan's timetable, allowing French armies critical time to prepare their defenses.

WORDS TO UNDERSTAND IN THIS CHAPTER

casualties—in war, military personnel killed, wounded, captured, or missing.

flank—the right or left side of a military formation.

offensive—a usually large military attack aimed at taking ground or gaining some strategic objective.

War Plans

Germany's strategy for fighting a two-front war against Russia and France was outlined in the Schlieffen Plan. It bore the stamp of two chiefs of the German General Staff. Alfred von Schlieffen devised the plan in 1905. His successor, Helmuth von Moltke, modified it up until the outbreak of World War I.

The Schlieffen Plan called for minimal forces to be assigned to the Eastern Front at the outset of the fighting. Russia's vast spaces and its underdeveloped railroad system would delay the concentration of troops at the front. Schlieffen believed that Russia would need 40 days before it could launch an effective attack. Moltke decided that one-fifth of Germany's available troops would be sufficient to keep the Russians at bay in the early weeks of the war.

The rest of the German army was to be deployed to the Western Front. France, according to Germany's war plans, would be defeated in about six weeks. Then the troops would be quickly transferred to the Eastern Front to dispatch Russia.

For Germany, everything hinged on a rapid victory in the west. The Germans could scarcely hope to win such a victory by means of a direct invasion across their border with France. They'd encounter fixed defenses as well as large concentrations of French troops. To avoid these obstacles, most of Germany's invading army would march through neutral countries—Belgium and tiny Luxembourg. After crossing into northeastern France, the Germans would wheel toward Paris.

France's war plan, known as Plan XVII, played into Germany's hands. Plan XVII called for a major *offensive* into the German regions of Alsace and Lorraine right after hostilities began. Meanwhile, France's border with Belgium would be left virtually undefended.

Belgian Resistance and the Battle of the Frontiers

Fortunately for the French, Germany encountered unexpected resistance in Belgium. Germany had demanded that its troops be permitted to march unmolested through Belgian territory. Belgium refused, electing to fight instead. It took the Germans more than two weeks, from August 4 to August 20, to overcome the outnumbered Belgians and begin moving into France. Surviving Belgian units pulled back to the fortress city of Antwerp, in northern Belgium.

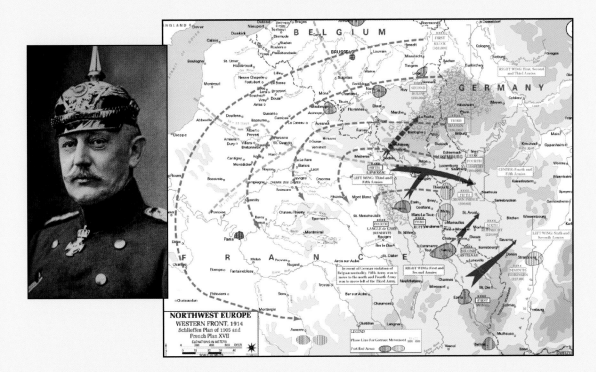

Count Helmuth von Moltke, chief of the General Staff of the German army (left), modified the Schlieffen Plan in the years leading up to the First World War. That plan called for the German army (pictured in red) to drive through Belgium and invade France.

In the meantime, about 100,000 British soldiers had been landed in France. The British Expeditionary Force (BEF) would take up position to the north of the French forces. It would prevent the Germans from sweeping around the French left *flank*.

On August 14, France began its large-scale invasion of Alsace and Lorraine. The offensive would eventually trigger four major battles: Lorraine, the Ardennes, Charleroi, and Mons. Together these engagements are known as the Battle of the Frontiers. More than a million French soldiers, and an equal number of Germans, would be brought into action during the fighting. So, too, would the BEF.

For several days, France's offensive progressed well. But on August 20, the Germans devastated France's Second Army—which occupied the French center—with long-range shelling. An infantry assault followed, sending most of the Second Army into retreat.

Over the next two days, the French launched two large attacks farther north, in Belgium. The attack in the Ardennes Forest and the attack around Charleroi, along the Sambre River, were both quickly repulsed. A hint of the carnage World War I would bring came on August 22. That day, about 27,000 French soldiers were killed at Ardennes and Charleroi.

The defeat at Charleroi left France's Fifth Army in danger of being overwhelmed. But on August 23, the BEF halted the advance of Germany's First Army—and protected the French left flank—at the Battle of Mons. Though outnumbered two to one, the British held a 20-mile stretch of the Mons-Condé Canal throughout the day. The French began a general retreat on August 24. The BEF followed.

The First Battle of the Marne

Buoyed by victory, the Germans drove forward relentlessly. In less than two weeks, they'd pushed 120 miles southwest from Mons. "We must allow the enemy no rest," one German commander exhorted, "until we have utterly defeated him on the whole front."

Such an outcome seemed possible as August gave way to September. The French and British continued to retreat. By September 4, the German right wing was just 30 miles east of Paris. Moltke ordered his right wing to halt there. The left wing, meanwhile, would attempt to encircle the French from the southeast.

But the French commander decided it was time for the Allies to go on the offensive. Marshal Joseph Joffre planned an attack against the German right, near the Marne River. It was slated to begin on September 6.

The First Battle of the Marne raged across a hundred-mile front for four days. At times, French forces seemed on the verge of collapsing. In the course of the battle, though, a large gap opened up between Germany's First and Second armies. French and British troops drove into that gap. Facing the threat of being rolled up on their flanks, the German commanders decided to withdraw. A general retreat northward began on September 10. The Germans would eventually pull back about 45 miles,

French civilians work in a vineyard as troops march toward the front lines during the First Battle of the Marne, September 1914.

The bolt-action rifle was the standard weapon for World War I infantry soldiers. Rifles were magazine fed, allowing soldiers to fire multiple rounds before reloading, but each spent cartridge had to be ejected manually by moving the bolt mechanism. Machine guns—which were too heavy to be carried by attacking soldiers—gave defenders a huge advantage in firepower.

digging entrenchments on high ground behind the Aisne River.

The Allies had suffered more than a quarter million *casualties*, including nearly 82,000 dead, at the Marne. But they'd finally stopped the enemy's advance. And in so doing, they'd dashed Germany's hopes of winning a quick war, as envisioned by the Schlieffen Plan.

A distraught Helmuth von Moltke, whom the Kaiser relieved of command, thought Germany's ultimate defeat was now inevitable. "We shall be crushed," Moltke predicted in a letter to his wife, "in the fight against East and West. . . . Our campaign is a cruel disillusion. And we shall have to pay for all the destruction which we have done."

On the Eastern Front

In late August, Russia had given German military leaders a bit of a shock. Less than three weeks after the outbreak of the war, two Russian armies had invaded East Prussia, the easternmost province of Germany.

The Russian plan was to press the outnumbered Germans from two directions. The Russian First Army would attack from the east. The Second Army would attack from the south. But the armies failed to coordinate their advances. They eventually became separated by too great a distance. If one were attacked, the other wouldn't be able to come to its aid.

The Germans massed their forces and surprised Russia's Second Army. The result was one of the most lopsided battles of the war. In the Battle of Tannenberg (August 26–30), about 50,000 Russian soldiers were killed, an additional 25,000 wounded, and 92,000 captured. Meanwhile, German casualties totaled only about 14,000, including fewer than 2,000 dead.

Having destroyed the Second Army, the Germans quickly turned their attention to the First. Between the 9th and 14th of September, they thrashed the Russians around the Masurian Lakes. Russia's invasion of East Prussia was finished.

The Russians fared better against Austria-Hungary. In a three-week series of engagements known as the Battles of Lemberg, Russian forces overran the strategic eastern part of Austria's Galicia territory. Austria-Hungary suffered some 400,000 casualties.

Russian soldiers captured by the Germans at Tannenberg pass through a border town on the way to detention camps in Germany. The German army could not follow up on its decisive victories at Tannenberg and the Masurian Lakes because the troops then had to reinforce Austro-Hungarian forces fighting in Galicia.

Emperor Franz Josef's troops were mauled even by tiny Serbia. Austria-Hungary's invasion of the kingdom, which began on August 12, was repelled in just a week.

In the fall of 1914, however, the ranks of the Central Powers grew significantly. On October 29, the Ottoman Empire—centered in Turkey—entered the war on the side of Germany and Austria-Hungary.

"Race to the Sea"

On the Western Front, the armies were engaged in a series of maneuvers dubbed "the Race to the Sea." That description is a bit misleading, as the movements were deliberate rather than rapid.

After the Germans entrenched behind the Aisne River following their retreat from the Marne, the French tried to dislodge them with a frontal attack. It failed.

The French next tried to outflank the Germans by moving forces to the north. The Germans followed suit. The flanking attempts sparked a series of clashes. But neither side succeeded in getting around or overrunning the other. Both sides dug defensive trenches.

With the failure of each successive flanking maneuver, the trench line extended further north. By mid-October, the only gap in the line was in Flanders, a low-lying region of Belgium that abuts the North Sea.

Retreating west from Antwerp, the remnants of Belgium's army—numbering just 65,000—made a heroic stand along the Yser River during the last two weeks of October. In part by opening floodgates that held back the North Sea, they stopped the Germans and secured a 20-mile line running inland from the coast.

Just to the south, around the city of Ypres, the Germans made one last push to break through. Thanks largely to the stalwart British, though, the Allies repelled the German offensive at the brutal First Battle of Ypres (October 19–November 22).

By the end of 1914, German and Allied trench lines faced each other across the entire 400-mile length of the Western Front, from the Belgian town of Nieuwpoort in the north to the border of neutral Switzerland in the south. Over the next four years, millions of lives would be expended in futile efforts to break through those lines.

 ## TEXT-DEPENDENT QUESTIONS

1. What was the Schlieffen Plan?
2. What was especially important about the First Battle of the Marne?
3. Where was the Ottoman Empire centered?

 ## RESEARCH PROJECT

In 1914, many German and British troops on the Western Front took a timeout from the war to celebrate Christmas. Beginning Christmas Eve, ordinary soldiers in the opposing trenches arranged a series of local, informal ceasefires. Use the Internet to research the so-called Christmas Truce. Write a one-page report that includes interesting details about the truce and, if possible, quotations from men who participated. What do you think the truce reveals about soldiers during the early months of the war?

THE VETERAN'S FAREWELL.

"Good Bye, my lad.
I only wish I were young enough
to go with you!"

ENLIST NOW!

Chapter 3

STALEMATE

As 1915 began, leaders in all the warring nations faced a sobering situation. A long conflict now appeared inevitable. Yet the armies had already incurred massive losses. France counted about a million soldiers killed, wounded, missing, or captured in 1914. Germany suffered more than 700,000 total casualties. Russian and Austro-Hungarian casualties also numbered in the hundreds of thousands. Britain's small army—which, unlike those of the other

In early 1915, many Europeans still viewed the war as a patriotic adventure. The English recruiting poster from that time (left) reflects this attitude, with an old man wistfully wishing a soldier good-bye. However, the grim reality of modern warfare soon wiped away such romantic ideas. The French and German posters are from 1918, and have darker overtones. The French poster (center) shows a soldier wearing a gas mask, while the German poster includes the ominous slogan, "Your Fatherland is in danger, register for the army!"

powers, was made up entirely of professional soldiers—had been decimated.

Manpower and Strategy

In the short term, the powers could replace their losses. For all except Britain, this meant drafting more men as necessary.

Fearing a public backlash against the war, British political leaders were reluctant to order *conscription*. A draft was finally instituted in 1916, as Britain faced a looming troop shortage. Before then, the ranks of the British army were filled exclusively by volunteers.

Dominion countries—nations that had been granted self-government within the British Empire—contributed troops to the Allied cause. These countries included Canada, Australia, New Zealand, and South Africa. Soldiers also came from the British colony of India. France, too, called up "Territorials" from its colonies in North Africa.

Colonists and native subjects were *mobilized* in Germany's four African colonies. But they served only in Africa, where Allied efforts to seize the German colonies led to brutal fighting.

The Allies and the Central Powers both had enormous pools of military-age males who could be conscripted. In neither case, of course, was the

 WORDS TO UNDERSTAND IN THIS CHAPTER

> *attrition*—the act of wearing down or exhausting a military force through constant harassment or attack.
>
> *conscription*—the drafting of citizens into military service.
>
> *division*—a large military unit capable of independent action.
>
> *mobilize*—to assemble troops for military duty.
>
> *no-man's-land*—the area between opposing front lines.
>
> *salient*—a bulge or outward projection of a defensive line.

pool of potential soldiers unlimited. And in the long term, the numbers decisively favored the Allies. That was because of Russia. With a population of about 166 million, Russia had more people than Germany, Austria-Hungary, and the Ottoman Empire combined.

Manpower considerations helped shape the evolving strategies of both sides. The Allies—and especially France and Britain on the Western Front—pursued a strategy of *attrition*. They intended to wear down German forces with repeated attacks.

Germany, meanwhile, focused on knocking Russia out of the war. Reserve units were sent to the Eastern Front. On the Western Front, the Germans would generally avoid offensive operations. As a rule, it takes fewer troops to defend a position than to attack one—and that would prove especially true in the trench warfare of World War I.

Blockades

Geography helped Germany and Austria-Hungary make up for the Allies' advantage in overall troop numbers. The two Central Powers had what military strategists call interior lines. They controlled the territory between the battle fronts. Using their railways, they could quickly move large numbers of soldiers from one front to another as circumstances warranted.

The flip side was that the Central Powers were effectively surrounded. Most critically, their enemies controlled the seas.

In late 1914, Britain initiated a naval blockade of Germany. By controlling access to the North Sea, the Royal Navy prevented Germany from importing raw materials and food.

German naval commanders were reluctant to risk their fleet in a decisive battle to break the British blockade. Germany's battleships remained bottled up in their North Sea bases.

But the German navy unleashed another weapon: the submarine, or U-boat. At the time, a submerged submarine was very difficult to detect, much less destroy.

During the first six months of the war, German U-boats had sunk a handful of British warships. In February 1915, though, Germany dramatically expanded the U-boat campaign. It declared the waters around the British Isles a war zone. Any vessel in those waters—including commercial ships from neutral nations—was subject to U-boat attack without warning.

Germany was trying to impose its own blockade. Britain seemed especially vulnerable, as it imported 60 percent of its food. But the German policy of unrestricted submarine warfare sparked an international outcry.

On May 7, 1915, a U-boat sank the British luxury liner *Lusitania* off the coast of Ireland. Nearly 1,200 men, women, and children lost their lives in the attack. One hundred twenty-eight were Americans.

Anti-German sentiment flared in the United States. President Woodrow Wilson was determined to maintain American neutrality. But Wilson demanded that Germany stop sinking unarmed ships without warning. The Germans agreed. They didn't want to risk provoking the United States into entering the war.

A German submarine, called a U-boat, rides through a rough sea. The German navy used U-boats to try to prevent food and war supplies from reaching its enemies, Great Britain and France. During the war U-boats sank nearly 5,000 Allied ships.

IN THE TRENCHES

During World War I, trenches were dug almost everywhere armies clashed. But nowhere did they assume more importance than on the Western Front. There, trench systems bred a four-year stalemate.

Trench construction varied considerably from one place to another, depending on factors such as soil type and topography. Nor was there any standard layout for trench systems. There were, however, some common features.

The frontline trench wasn't built in a straight line but had frequent bends or zigzags. This would limit casualties to a short section of the trench if an artillery shell hit. It would also prevent attacking soldiers from firing down the length of the line if they got into the trench. A belt of barbed wire in front of the trench provided another obstacle to a successful attack.

Behind the frontline trench, usually at a distance of several hundred yards, was the support trench. It held men and supplies that could be moved quickly to the frontline trench if needed. Behind the support trench was the reserve trench. It held units that would counterattack if the other trench lines were overrun. Communications trenches connected the trench lines, allowing men to move back and forth under cover.

Units cycled in and out of the trenches. They did stints in the frontline, support, and reserve trenches before being sent to the rear for rest.

Terror and misery abounded in the trenches. Even when a sector was relatively quiet, frontline troops knew they could be killed at any time by an artillery shell or, if they were careless, by a sniper's bullet. Trenches afforded little protection from the cold during winter. They flooded after rainstorms. They were infested by rats, some of which grew to the size of cats by feasting on unburied corpses in **no-man's-land** (as the area between opposing trenches was called). Lice and poor sanitation, combined with the cramped conditions, spread disease.

A New Weapon

Unrestricted submarine warfare was a violation of international law. So, for that matter, was the British blockade of Germany. Food was supposed to be exempt from blockades.

Another shocking violation of international law—this one coming at the Second Battle of Ypres—underscored the brutality of the Great War. On April 22, 1915, German forces opened more than 5,700 cylinders of chlorine gas they'd placed opposite the *Salient*, a bulge in the Allied trench line east of Ypres. A gentle breeze carried the resulting yellowish green fog into a section of the Allied line held by some 10,000 French Territorial troops. Within minutes, about half of the men had died in agony. Moisture in their respiratory tract had reacted with the gas to form hydrochloric acid. That ate away at the lining of the windpipe and lungs, causing violent coughing, spasms, and a buildup of fluid. Death resulted from asphyxiation. A gas-attack survivor likened the experience "to drowning only on dry land."

Not all the French Territorial soldiers at Ypres had inhaled a fatal concentration of gas. Those who were able to move fled their trenches in panic. But many of the men couldn't see—chlorine gas can cause temporary blindness—and the Germans gunned them down by the hundreds.

The gas attack had completely cleared a four-mile stretch of Allied trenches—and with virtually no German casualties. Two days later, on April 24, the Germans launched another gas attack at Ypres. This one inflicted heavy casualties on Canadian troops.

But the Allies quickly adapted to gas attacks. Frontline soldiers were soon outfitted with simple cloth respirators, as well as goggles to protect their eyes. Improved gas masks would follow.

The Allies lost ground in the Second Battle of Ypres, Germany's only offensive on the Western Front in 1915. But the Germans failed to capture Ypres in the month-long battle.

The main significance of the Second Battle of Ypres is that it opened the way for the widespread use of poison gas. Within a few months, the

This aerial photo shows a French poison gas attack directed against German trenches in Belgium. Soldiers caught without gas masks were killed or debilitated.

Allies were using chlorine gas against the Germans. By the end of 1915, Germany had deployed phosgene, which was more difficult to detect, and deadlier, than chlorine gas. The Allies followed suit. Artillery shells replaced cylinders as the means of delivering gas. In 1917, Germany introduced mustard gas. It caused painful blisters on exposed flesh or, if inhaled, in the lungs. By war's end, more than 90,000 men had been killed by poison gas. More than a million had been wounded, and many of them would be sick or disabled for the rest of their lives.

New Fronts

French and British forces mounted several offensives on the Western Front in 1915. These included campaigns in the Champagne, Artois, and Vosges areas. Overall, the Allies made minimal gains—if they made any gains at all—and casualties were heavy.

In April 1915, another nation agreed to join the Allies. At the outset of the war, Italy had declined to its honor its pact with Germany and Austria-Hungary. The prospect of gaining territory from Austria-Hungary eventually convinced Italian leaders to take up the Allied cause. But Italy's military efforts would prove an exercise in futility. Italian forces attacked repeatedly along the Isonzo River and in the rugged mountains separating Italy from Austria-Hungary. Time after time, Austro-Hungarian troops holding higher ground sent the Italians reeling.

Further to the east, the Allies had opened another offensive. The target was the Turkish Straits, three connected waterways linking the Black Sea to the Mediterranean. With control of the straits, the Allies could ship much-needed supplies to Russia. They could also destroy the Ottoman capital, Constantinople (Istanbul), and perhaps knock the Ottoman Empire out of the war.

Initially, the Allies tried to force their way through the straits with naval power alone. When that failed, Allied commanders decided on an invasion of the Gallipoli Peninsula. It bounds the narrow Dardanelles—the southernmost section of the Turkish Straits—to the northwest.

On April 25, 1915, Allied troops landed at Gallipoli. British forces (soon to be joined by French units) went ashore near the southern tip of the peninsula. Soldiers from the Australia and New Zealand Army Corps (ANZAC) landed in an especially rugged area about 10 miles to the north. It would be dubbed Anzac Cove.

The Allies managed to gain toeholds in both landing zones. But determined Turkish troops, fighting from high ground, prevented them from advancing.

Both sides dug in, and both received a flood of reinforcements. A brutal stalemate ensued. In the ANZAC zone, enemy trenches were separated by as little as 10 yards—close enough to toss grenades.

In August, the British landed three fresh *divisions* at Suvla Bay, north of Anzac Cove. But that failed to break the deadlock.

Allied forces began withdrawing from the Gallipoli Peninsula in late November, with the last troops evacuated on January 8, 1916. Estimates of the total number of Allied casualties in the eight-month campaign range as high as a quarter million, with more than 44,000 dead. Turkish losses are also believed to have totaled about 250,000, including more than 86,000 dead.

Russians and Serbians Routed

In the late spring of 1915, the Central Powers won a major victory against Russia. On May 2, German and Austro-Hungarian forces overwhelmed the Russian lines between the towns of Gorlice and Tarnów, in southern Poland. After smashing two Russian divisions brought up to plug the gap, they broke into open territory.

By late June, when the Gorlice-Tarnów campaign wound down, the Central Powers had recaptured most of Galicia. In July, they pressed the attack in Russian-controlled Poland, winning a string of victories.

Australian troops charge a Turkish trench on the Gallipoli Peninsula, 1915. The Gallipoli landing resulted in many casualties on both sides during eight months of fighting before the Allied armies were forced to withdraw.

Facing the collapse of their entire front, the Russians abandoned Poland. Pursued by German forces, they retreated east. Finally, in late September, the Russians were able to establish a defensive line. In the five months since the beginning of the Gorlice-Tarnów campaign, a million Russian soldiers had been taken prisoner. Nearly a million others had been killed or wounded.

For the time being at least, Russia no longer posed any threat to the Central Powers. And that was bad news for Serbia. Germany's Eleventh Army was transferred from the Eastern Front. Along with divisions from Austria-Hungary, it invaded Serbia from the north in October 1915. Meanwhile, Bulgaria—which had been enticed to join the Central Powers with the promise of receiving Serbian territory—launched an attack from the east. By December, the Serbian army had been routed. Survivors fled into Montenegro and Albania.

TEXT-DEPENDENT QUESTIONS

1. To what did the term *no-man's-land* refer?
2. What is phosgene?
3. Where is the Gallipoli Peninsula? What did the Allies hope to accomplish by taking it?

RESEARCH PROJECT

The horrors spawned by World War I weren't confined to the battlefield. Civilians, too, suffered enormously. Sometimes the harm they endured was unintended, but sometimes they were deliberately targeted. Perhaps no episode was more notorious (or remains more controversial today) than the Ottoman Empire's treatment of its Armenian minority. Use the Internet to find out what happened to the Armenians of Turkey beginning in April 1915. Write a one-page report.

Chapter 4

THE SLAUGHTER CONTINUES

On Christmas Day in 1915, Erich von Falkenhayn sent a letter to Kaiser Wilhelm. In it, Falkenhayn—chief of the German General Staff—outlined a plan for ending the war on the Western Front. Falkenhayn didn't think it possible for Germany to break through the

French soldiers attack a German defensive position, 1916. By this time the conflict in Europe had become a stalemate, with hundreds of miles of strongly defended trenches on each side making it nearly impossible for military units to gain a significant advantage.

> ## 📖 WORDS TO UNDERSTAND IN THIS CHAPTER
>
> *battalion*—a large group of infantry soldiers, usually between 500 and 1,000, commanded by a lieutenant colonel.
>
> *mop-up operations*—operations after a battle is over to root out any remaining enemy forces or installations.

Allied lines. But he also didn't think it necessary. Instead, Falkenhayn proposed to draw France into a battle it couldn't win but wouldn't abandon, a battle in which German artillery would decimate *battalion* after battalion of French reserves. As Germany was "bleeding white the French army," the British would be pressured to launch an ill-considered offensive. Germany would crush it. Demoralized, France would give up. Britain's exit from the war would then be just a matter of time.

Falkenhayn's plan won the enthusiastic approval of the Kaiser. Preparations were soon under way to bleed the French white at Verdun.

The Battle for Verdun

Verdun had a long history and held great national significance for the French. A system of fortifications was supposed to protect the city. But the heavy guns had been removed for use elsewhere.

The French lines at Verdun formed a salient, making it possible for the Germans to bring artillery to bear from three sides. They gathered about 1,200 artillery pieces for the attack. Shortly after 7 A.M. on February 21, 1916, the big guns opened up. The Battle of Verdun had begun.

The first days of the battle unfolded much as Falkenhayn had hoped. His artillery devastated the French lines. German infantry units advanced several miles. They encountered little resistance. French leaders, deciding that Verdun must be held at all costs, brought up large numbers of reinforcements.

THE WAR IN THE MIDDLE EAST

At the outset of World War I, the British had two overriding concerns in the Middle East. One was to protect their access to oil, which powered the Royal Navy's ships. The other was to protect the Suez Canal, through which troops and supplies from India, Australia, and New Zealand moved to reach the Western Front.

By November 1914, British forces had defeated Ottoman troops and captured Basra, in southern Mesopotamia (modern-day Iraq). This meant the British could get oil from Persia (Iran). In Egypt, the British fended off an Ottoman attack on the Suez Canal in early 1915, and had essentially eliminated any threat to the waterway by mid-1916.

Having secured their main strategic objectives in the Middle East, the British focused on conquering Ottoman-controlled territory. In Mesopotamia, British forces suffered a costly defeat at Kut but eventually succeeded in driving up the Tigris River to capture Baghdad. On the Arabian Peninsula, the British supported a 1916 Arab revolt against Ottoman rule. And, beginning in 1917, British forces drove east from Egypt into Palestine. By the end of the war, British troops were in control of the territory that today makes up Israel, Jordan, Lebanon, and Syria.

Falkenhayn had believed that the German artillery would shred Verdun's defenders. Since the infantry would be needed mostly for *mop-up operations*, German casualties would be minimal.

But the French displayed incredible fortitude at Verdun. Battered French units repulsed the German infantry sent to finish them off. The French artillery was organized and brought into action. It exacted a heavy toll on German troops. Desperate fighting raged week after week. Both sides were being bled white.

Slaughter at the Somme

French leaders pleaded with the British to begin a planned offensive early, in order to take pressure off Verdun. Sir Douglas Haig, the British commander-in-chief, agreed. The offensive would occur at the Somme River, about 125 miles northwest of Verdun. Twenty British divisions, joined by five French divisions, would participate.

On June 24, 1916, the Allies began a massive artillery barrage. Over the next week, about 3,000 guns relentlessly bombarded German positions along a 20-mile front. In all, more than 1.5 million shells were fired.

Haig was sure this bombardment had destroyed the German defenses and annihilated the defenders. He anticipated an easy advance by British infantry. Then, cavalry units would race ahead to strike the enemy far to the rear.

British officers seemed to share their commander's confidence. "You will find the Germans all dead," one infantry officer assured his men. "Not even a rat will have survived."

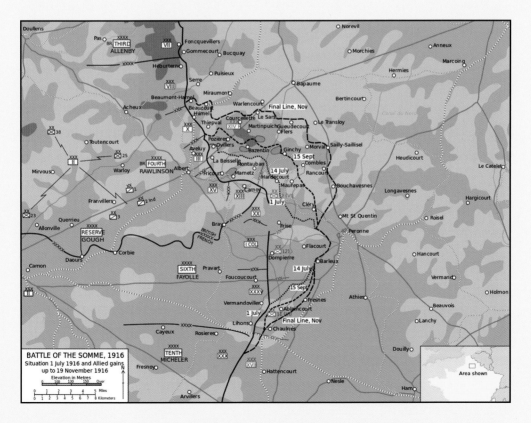

This map of the Somme battlefield shows the British forces (in blue) gradually pushing back German forces (black line) between July and November 1916. The Allied gains were marginal, given the high casualty rate suffered during the Somme campaign.

In fact, the German defenses at the Somme were much more formidable than the British suspected. The Germans had excavated a system of bunkers beneath and behind their trenches. German troops waited out the Allied bombardment 30 feet underground.

At 7:30 A.M. on July 1, Allied troops climbed out of their frontline trenches and poured into no-man's-land. Following orders from General Haig, British soldiers advanced slowly and in neat lines. Advancing ahead of them was a "creeping barrage" of protective fire laid down by the British field artillery.

When that barrage receded, German soldiers scrambled out of their dugouts. In front of them, in some cases only 30 or 40 yards away, was a sea of British troops. Barbed wire stopped many from advancing further, however. Haig and his staff had erroneously assumed the artillery bombardment would destroy the wire. Now, German machine gun crews quickly set up their weapons and opened fire. From the rear, German artillery began shelling no-man's-land.

The result was wholesale slaughter. Of approximately 100,000 British soldiers who went forward on July 1, nearly 20,000 were killed, and 40,000 others were wounded. It was—and remains to this day—the highest single-day casualty count in British military history.

Yet Haig was undeterred. Insisting that the Germans had been "shaken," he continued the offensive in the days and weeks that followed. The Allies made paltry gains in territory at a huge cost in dead and wounded.

On September 15, the British introduced a new weapon at the Somme: the tank. German troops were initially stunned by the appearance of the ironclad behemoths. But the tanks were prone to mechanical failure, and coordinated tank and infantry tactics had yet to be developed. Though tanks would prove effective in later battles, at the Somme they made little difference.

Heavy rains finally brought an end to the Battle of the Somme in November. The British had suffered about 420,000 total casualties, the French about 200,000. German casualties may have reached half a million.

The fighting at Verdun, meanwhile, dragged on. When it ended, in mid-December, the lines were around the same place they'd been at the start of the battle 10 months earlier. But more than 300,000 men had lost their lives, and about 750,000 had been wounded.

Losses on the Battlefield, Unrest on the Home Front

Verdun and the Somme weren't the only notable battles of 1916. On May 31, the British and German navies clashed in the North Sea, off the coast of Denmark. In all, 250 ships and about 100,000 men saw action, making the Battle of Jutland the largest naval engagement in history up to that point.

The Royal Navy suffered greater losses in the battle. Fourteen of His Majesty's ships were sent to the bottom, and nearly 6,100 British sailors lost their lives. Germany, meanwhile, had 11 ships sunk and about 2,550

German sailors clamber onto the side of a German cruiser that is sinking in the North Sea. The Battle of Jutland in 1916 was the largest naval battle of the war. Both sides claimed victory: the Germans sank more British ships, but the British were able to maintain their blockade of German ports.

men killed. But the Germans failed to break Britain's control of the North Sea, so the British blockade remained in force.

That blockade would exact an increasingly severe toll on German civilians. During the winter of 1916–17, food and fuel shortages claimed the lives of tens of thousands. Germans who'd once enthusiastically supported the war began turning against it. "Our thoughts are chiefly taken up with wondering what our next meal will be," one woman wrote in January 1917, "and dreaming of the good things that once existed. . . . The truth is, the soul of the people is sick unto death of the useless carnage and hateful sinfulness of it all."

Such feelings weren't limited to Germany. In Russia, discontent with the war would help lead to the overthrow of the tsar.

In March 1917, a revolution in Russia forced Tsar Nicholas II (1868-1918) to turn control of the empire over to a provisional government.

In early June 1916, Russia had launched a massive offensive. By the standards of World War I, the Brusilov Offensive was quite successful. Over the course of three months, Russian forces gained a significant amount of territory along a 250-mile front in Poland and Galicia. In some places, the Russians drove more than 50 miles. They also shattered Austria-Hungary's army, which suffered total casualties estimated at three-quarters of a million. This included 400,000 prisoners.

But the successes of the Brusilov Offensive had come at a cost of more than a million Russians killed, wounded, or captured. After two years of horrendous—and steadily mounting—casualties, the ranks of the Russian army churned with resentment. Anger rose on the home front as well. The loss of husbands, fathers, and sons was compounded by serious food shortages and a collapsing economy.

In March 1917, riots and worker strikes broke out in St. Petersburg. The unrest quickly spread to other cities. Many Russian troops joined the protests.

On March 15, Tsar Nicholas II was forced to abdicate (give up the throne). Members of Russia's parliament, the Duma, formed a provisional (temporary) government. It planned to keep Russia in the war.

Enter, the United States

From the outbreak of hostilities through 1916, the U.S. government had maintained an official policy of neutrality in World War I. That policy was broadly popular with the American public. Indeed, President Woodrow Wilson won reelection in November 1916 with the campaign slogan "He Kept Us Out of the War." Within a few months, however, American public opinion would undergo a dramatic shift, and Wilson would decide that neutrality was no longer possible.

In the face of the crippling British blockade, Germany resumed unrestricted submarine warfare in February 1917. German leaders recognized that the sinking of American merchant ships, or passenger ships carrying American citizens, might draw the United States into the war. But that was a risk they were willing to take. They believed Britain could be brought to its knees in a few months, before enough American troops had arrived on the Western Front to make a difference.

Germany also had a plan for keeping U.S. forces occupied at home. In a diplomatic message known as the Zimmerman Telegram, Germany's foreign minister proposed an alliance with Mexico. If Mexico agreed to attack the United States, Germany would provide generous financial aid, and it would support the transfer of Texas, New Mexico, and Arizona to Mexico.

Unfortunately for Germany, the British intercepted, decoded, and provided the U.S. government a copy of the Zimmerman Telegram. News of the German proposal sparked a firestorm of outrage in the United States. On April 6, 1917, Congress overwhelmingly approved President Wilson's request for a declaration of war against Germany.

TEXT-DEPENDENT QUESTIONS

1. What new weapon was introduced at the Battle of the Somme?
2. Name some factors that led to the fall of Russia's Tsar Nicholas II.
3. What was the Zimmerman Telegram?

RESEARCH PROJECT

"This war could not have been fought, either by the other nations engaged or by America, if it had not been for the services of the women," President Wilson said in late 1918. Research how women supported the war effort. What new roles did they take on? See if you can find some first-hand accounts of women's wartime experiences (for example, in diaries or autobiographies). Write a brief report on one aspect of women and World War I you find especially interesting.

Chapter 5

WINNING THE WAR, LOSING THE PEACE

In April 1917, the United States had fewer than 215,000 soldiers and marines in uniform. That certainly wasn't enough men to turn the tide in World War I. But American troop strength would increase

American soldiers attack German defensive positions during an offensive near the Marne. The arrival of large numbers of U.S. soldiers in Europe during 1918 helped to turn the war decisively in the Allies' favor.

WORDS TO UNDERSTAND IN THIS CHAPTER

armistice—a temporary cessation of hostilities; truce.

doughboy—slang term for an American soldier or marine during World War I.

dramatically as a result of the military draft authorized by Congress and through voluntary enlistments.

British and French commanders expected American troops to deploy to the trenches immediately upon arriving in France. They also expected the *doughboys*, as the Americans were called, to be incorporated into existing British and French units.

General John "Black Jack" Pershing, commander-in-chief of the American Expeditionary Force (AEF), had other ideas. Pershing insisted that the AEF operate independently. But outfitting and training enough troops to make that possible would take time. Pershing's doughboys, in fact, wouldn't see significant action until 1918. In the meantime, the Allies faced several crises.

Men at Their Limits

The Allies planned a major spring offensive on the Western Front for April 1917. The main thrust of the offensive would come near the Aisne River. Following a two-week artillery bombardment, 800,000 French troops were to overrun German positions along a 50-mile front.

The architect of the offensive was General Robert Nivelle. He'd been elevated to commander-in-chief of French forces in late 1916. Nivelle was sure his offensive would smash the enemy and end the war. In fact, he confidently predicted that Germany would ask for surrender terms within 48 hours of the French attack. And Nivelle projected French casualties to total just 10,000.

The Second Battle of the Aisne began on the morning of April 16. It was clear almost immediately that Nivelle's rosy predictions wouldn't come to pass. The Germans had adopted a "defense in depth" strategy. They'd left their front lines virtually undefended. Behind that, to a distance of more than five miles, the Germans had set up a web of concrete bunkers, pillboxes, and machine-gun nests. Nivelle's artillery bombardment had left most of those defenses intact. French troops advanced at a horrendous cost. Forty thousand were killed by April 18.

Yet Nivelle refused to reconsider his plan. He canceled all scheduled leave. "The hour of sacrifice has arrived," he informed the troops.

In those words, one corporal noted, many French troops "heard nothing but another terrible threat: new suffering, great dangers, the prospect of an awful death in a vain and useless sacrifice, because no one trusted the outcome of this new butchery."

French soldiers had reached their limit. On May 5, France's 21st Division disobeyed orders to attack along the blood-soaked Chemin des Dames

 ## OF WAR AND FREE SPEECH

By 1917, most Americans supported U.S. entry into World War I. Still, a significant antiwar movement existed in the country. It drew support from certain labor organizations, women's groups, and intellectuals.

The U.S. government took highly controversial action to stifle opposition to the war. At the urging of President Wilson, Congress passed the Espionage Act of 1917. In 1918, Congress passed the Sedition Act. These laws curtailed freedom of speech. They made it a crime to publicly express "disloyal" or "abusive" opinions about the U.S. government, to encourage opposition to the draft, or to say, write, or publish anything the president deemed "useful to the enemy."

More than a thousand Americans were prosecuted under the two acts. The laws were repealed in 1921.

Ridge. Other units followed suit. Mutiny swept through the French army. Soldiers refused to attack—or even to move to the front lines.

On May 15, Nivelle was relieved of command. His replacement, General Philippe Pétain, gradually extinguished the revolt. One way he did so was by promising he'd refrain from any major new offensives.

Suffering and Setbacks

Had Germany's military leaders found out about the French mutiny, the results could have been disastrous. In part to draw attention away from the weakened French lines, British Empire forces launched an offensive in Flanders on July 31. The Battle of Passchendaele, also known as the Third Battle of Ypres, would be fought amid mud so deep men and horses drowned. By November, when the battle ended, the Allies had expanded the Ypres salient five miles in places. But Allied casualties totaled an estimated 325,000. The Germans suffered about a quarter million casualties.

Meanwhile, German and Austro-Hungarian forces had smashed Italy's army at the Battle of Caporetto, also called the Twelfth Battle of the Isonzo. More than 280,000 Italian soldiers surrendered during the battle, which lasted from late October to mid-November. In the wake of that disaster, France and Britain dispatched 11 divisions to the region to ensure that Italy remained in the war.

Exit, Russia

For the Allies, the situation on the Eastern Front was even more discouraging. On July 1, 1917, Russia had begun an ill-considered offensive in Galicia. The Kerensky Offensive, named for the Provisional Government's minister of war, saw some early gains. But after a few days the offensive foundered. Russian troops refused to fight. They deserted in large numbers. By the end of July, a counterattack by German and Austro-Hungarian forces had driven the Russian lines back 150 miles.

Angry Russians storm the Winter Palace in St. Petersburg, Russia, in October 1917. The second revolution in Russia during 1917 resulted in the establishment of the Communist Bolshevik government, which soon made peace with Germany—a serious blow to the Allies.

The defeat helped undermine the already weak Provisional Government. In November, a radical group called the Bolsheviks seized power. In December, the Bolshevik government signed an **armistice** (truce) with the Central Powers. Russia's surrender was formalized in the Treaty of Brest-Litovsk, signed on March 3, 1918.

With no enemy now to the east, Germany was able to transfer half a million troops to the Western Front. Germany's top generals, Erich Ludendorff and Paul von Hindenburg, saw one last chance to win the war. German forces would have to defeat the Allies before U.S. troops were fully deployed.

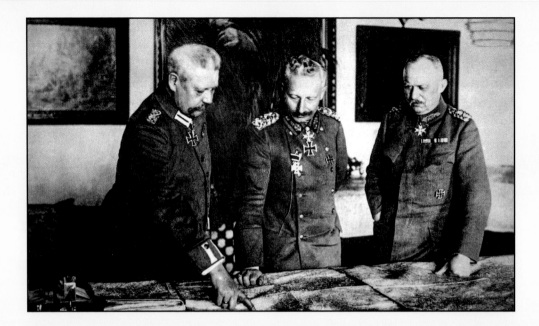

Generals Paul von Hindenburg (left) and Erich Ludendorff (right) discuss plans for a German offensive with Kaiser Wilhelm. The two generals' successes on the Eastern Front during 1914 and 1915 had resulted in their being placed in charge of the German military effort.

The "Emperor's Battle"

Ludendorff planned a series of spring offensives code-named the *Kaiserschlacht* ("Kaiser's Battle"). They emphasized rapid movement.

On the morning of March 21, German artillery pounded a 50-mile section of the Allied front near the Somme. The intensity of the bombardment was astounding: more than a million shells exploded in just five hours. In the assault that followed, German forces opened a huge breach around the town of Saint-Quentin. Britain's Fifth Army buckled and collapsed. To the south of Saint-Quentin, France's Sixth Army was compelled to pull back.

Ludendorff hoped to wheel his forces northwest and drive the British to the North Sea. But after a few days of spectacular advances, the German offensive began to lose momentum. Still, by the time the offensive in the Somme ended on April 5, the Germans had managed to drive the Allies back 40 miles in places.

In the early days of the offensive, French forces had been slow to come to the aid of the reeling British. This helped convince Allied leaders of the need for closer coordination. As a result, the French general Ferdinand Foch was appointed the Allies' supreme commander. General Pershing quickly abandoned his insistence that the AEF operate independently. American troops, too, would be placed under Foch's overall command.

From April to July 1918, the Germans launched four more offensives. Of these, two once again produced significant gains in territory: the Battle of the Lys, in Flanders (April 9–29), and the Third Battle of the Aisne

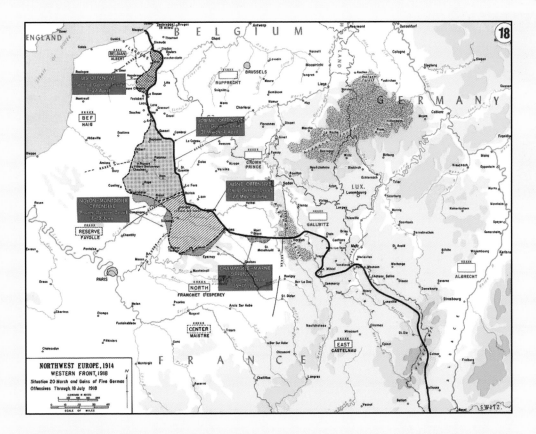

In March 1918, Germany launched attacks at critical points along the Western Front, hoping to force France and Britain to surrender before large numbers of U.S. troops could reach the battlefield. Although the Spring Offensive succeeded in gaining control over some French territory by July, the German military suffered too many casualties to hold the ground for long.

(May 27–June 6). The offensives of Noyon-Montdidier (June 9–13) and the Champagne-Marne (July 15–17) were less successful.

All told, Ludendorff's 1918 offensives had inflicted more than 850,000 casualties on the Allies. But Germany had suffered some 700,000 casualties of its own. Most important, the *Kaiserschlacht* hadn't knocked Britain or France out of the war—and American troops were now arriving in great numbers.

Doughboys had already made a difference. In late May, German units smashed the French in the Aisne. They pushed quickly toward the Marne. Paris was just 40 miles away, and victory seemed within Germany's grasp. But in early June, the U.S. 3rd Division stopped the Germans at Château-Thierry. At nearby Belleau Wood, U.S. Marines beat back waves of attackers, effectively bringing the German offensive to an end. Then, in three weeks of savage fighting, the Marines pushed the Germans out of Belleau Wood.

Final Battles

On July 18, French and American forces counterattacked along the Marne. That marked the start of what would come to be called the Hundred Days Offensive. For the remainder of the summer and into autumn, the Allies would maintain constant pressure on the Western Front.

On August 8, British Empire forces spearheaded a well-coordinated tank and infantry assault that smashed through the German lines at the Battle of Amiens. Twelve thousand German troops surrendered in a single day, and the effect on German morale was profound. Erich Ludendorff called it "the blackest day of the German Army in the war."

By the beginning of September, German troops had retreated behind the Hindenburg Line, the position from which they had begun the *Kaiserschlacht* in March. Constructed between late 1916 and early 1917, the Hindenburg Line was a series of formidable defenses. It stretched from near the city of Arras in the north to the Aisne River in the south.

On September 12, the American Expeditionary Force—under the

African-American soldiers served in racially segregated units during World War I. One such unit, the 369th Infantry Regiment, won acclaim for its toughness, bravery, and determination. Nicknamed the Harlem Hellfighters, the 369th Infantry was among the most decorated U.S. combat units of the war.

command of General Pershing—began its first major independent offensive. The target was the St. Mihiel salient, between Verdun and Nancy. In a four-day battle, the AEF prevailed, chasing German forces out of an area they'd held since 1914.

There was little time for the doughboys to rest. Pershing had committed to launching another massive offensive, 60 miles to the north, on September 26. That assault would be part of what Allied commander-in-chief Ferdinand Foch envisioned as a "grand offensive." As the AEF and French divisions under Pershing's command attacked between the Meuse River and the Argonne Forest, other Allied armies would strike at the Hindenburg Line and in Flanders. In all, more than 90 Allied divisions would be involved in Foch's grand offensive. The Germans, he believed, didn't have enough men to stop that onslaught.

The Meuse-Argonne sector was a difficult area in which to mount an offensive. Rugged hills and dense woods hampered communication. In

The U.S. 18th Infantry passes through the ruins of a French village on their way to the front at St. Mihiel, September 1918.

many places, tanks couldn't be used, and advancing troops would be funneled into narrow ravines. German forces had spent four years constructing and refining defenses. All these factors—plus the inexperience of the doughboys—led to high American casualties. But Pershing and his troops pressed on with grim determination. In seven weeks, they advanced more than 30 miles. Of about 1.2 million doughboys who fought in the Meuse-Argonne Offensive, more than 26,000 lost their lives. An additional 95,000 were wounded.

But Foch's grand offensive succeeded. By the second week of October, the Allies had overwhelmed the Hindenburg Line. Allied forces were on the move in Belgium as well. Throughout the rest of the month, Germans retreated across land they'd conquered in 1914.

On October 30—a month after Bulgaria had ended its participation in the war—Ottoman Turkey signed an armistice with the Allies. When Austria-Hungary signed an armistice on November 3, Germany had no allies left.

Germans, too, had lost their appetite for continuing the war. In late October, Germany's naval high command issued orders for the fleet to steam out of port and engage the Royal Navy. But sailors in Wilhelmshaven and Kiel mutinied. Unrest quickly spread to other German cities, with sailors, soldiers, and workers demanding not just an end to the war but also political reforms.

On November 9, Kaiser Wilhelm abdicated. Two days later, Germany signed an armistice with the Allies. At 11:00 A.M. on November 11, 1918, the guns finally fell silent.

Aftermath

The significance of World War I is hard to overstate. The conflict swept away four empires: Russian, Austro-Hungarian, German, and Ottoman. In the war's aftermath, boundaries were redrawn in Europe, the Middle East, and Africa. Colonies changed hands, and new countries were created.

The First World War ranks among the bloodiest conflicts in human history, though the exact toll cannot be known. Most historians today believe that at least 8.5 million military personnel lost their lives, and about 21 million were wounded. Up to 7 million civilians also died as a result of the war.

Every war destroys things—property, lives, dreams. World War I also claimed something else: faith in the progress of human civilization. Across Europe, in victorious nations as well as vanquished ones, disillusionment ran deep. It stemmed not simply from the scale of the carnage or the widespread belief that leaders had lied to and manipulated their citizens. There was also a pervasive feeling that, in the end, the war had been pointless.

In August 1914, the British author H. G. Wells had written an essay (soon expanded into a book) titled "The War That Will End War." In it, Wells declared, "Every soldier who fights against Germany now is a crusader against war. . . . This, the greatest of all wars, is not just another war—it is the last war!"

During the early stages of the conflict, many people in Britain found inspiration in the idea that they were engaged in a "war to end all wars." In 1917, President Wilson offered a similarly idealistic reason for the United States to enter the war. The world, he said, had to be "made safe for democracy." Wilson later issued a set of aims—known as the Fourteen

The leaders of the major Allied powers included (left to right) David Lloyd George of Great Britain, Orlando Vittorio of Italy, Georges Clemenceau of France, and Woodrow Wilson of the United States. Known as the "Big Four," they oversaw a peace conference in Paris that lasted for six months in 1919. The peace conference resulted in the breakup of the defeated Austro-Hungarian and Ottoman empires, which created many new countries. It also imposed punitive terms on Germany. Within two decades, resentment over the Treaty of Versailles would result in another world war.

Points—that he believed could serve as the foundation for a lasting peace. They included worldwide arms reduction, greater self-determination for colonized peoples, and the creation of an "association of nations" to resolve international disputes peacefully.

Wilson believed that the defeated Central Powers should be treated fairly. But at the Paris Peace Conference, which opened in January 1919, French and British determination to punish Germany carried the day. Under the Treaty of Versailles, signed June 28, 1919, Germany was forced to accept sole blame for starting World War I. It was also obliged to make payments, mostly to France and Belgium, for war damages. In Germany, these and other terms of the treaty caused great anger and bred social and political instability. That helped pave the way for the eventual rise of Adolf Hitler and the Nazi Party.

The Nazi regime was brutal and totalitarian—that is, it sought to control every aspect of citizens' lives. The communist government of the Soviet Union—which replaced Russia—was also brutal and totalitarian.

Nor was the world "made safe for democracy" elsewhere. For example, Britain and France carved up former Ottoman territories in the Middle East with little regard for the will of the people living there. In the process, they sowed the seeds of conflicts that persist to this day.

Of course, the most terrible conflict birthed by the "war to end all wars" was World War II. Sparked by Nazi aggression, it erupted in 1939, just 20 years after the signing of the Treaty of Versailles.

In World War I, more than 116,000 Americans had been killed, and 204,000 wounded. While the United States emerged from the war as a rising economic power, most Americans came to oppose further U.S. involvement in international politics. The association of nations that President Wilson had championed was, in fact, created under the Treaty of Versailles. It was called the League of Nations. But the United States never joined the League, as the U.S. Senate refused to ratify the Treaty of Versailles. American isolationism would be ended only by the coming of the Second World War.

TEXT-DEPENDENT QUESTIONS

1. What was the *Kaiserschlacht*?
2. What major offensive did the American Expeditionary Force spearhead in 1918?
3. What treaty was signed on June 28, 1919?

RESEARCH PROJECT

Soldiers from about 20 countries fought in World War I. Compile a list of these combatant nations. Then gather the following data for each: number of troops mobilized; number of troops killed; number of troops wounded. (Remember: the figures will be estimates, so note your sources.) Present the information in graphic form (for example, bar graphs or pie charts).

CHRONOLOGY

1914

June - Archduke Franz Ferdinand, heir to the throne of Austria-Hungary, is assassinated on June 28.

July - Germany pledges to support Austria-Hungary in the event Russia intervenes in a war against Serbia. Austria-Hungary declares war on Serbia (July 28).

August - War declarations bring Germany, Russia, France, and Britain into the conflict. German forces advance through Belgium and push into France. German forces smash a Russian army at the Battle of Tannenberg.

September - Allied forces halt the German drive toward Paris at the First Battle of the Marne. The Germans entrench behind the Aisne River.

October - The First Battle of Ypres begins on Oct. 19; by the time it ends about a month later, trench lines extend across the length of the Western Front. The Ottoman Empire enters the war on the side of the Central Powers (Oct. 29).

1915

February - Germany begins unrestricted submarine warfare around British Isles.

April - German forces introduce poison gas at the Second Battle of Ypres. Allied troops land in Gallipoli. Italy joins the Allies.

May - The Central Powers' successful Gorlice-Tarnów campaign begins. A German U-boat torpedoes and sinks the passenger liner Lusitania.

October - The Central Powers launch a successful invasion of Serbia.

1916

February - The Battle of Verdun begins; it will last until late December.

May - The British and German navies fight the Battle of Jutland.

June - Russia launches the Brusilov Offensive, which makes significant territorial gains but at a high cost in casualties. On the Arabian Peninsula, Arabs begin a revolt against Ottoman rule, which the British encourage.

July - The Battle of the Somme (July 1–Nov. 18) begins. The British introduce the tank during this battle.

1917

March - Riots and worker strikes rock St. Petersburg and other Russian cities. On the 15th, Tsar Nicholas II abdicates. Russia's Provisional Government is formed.

April - On April 6, following revelations about the Zimmerman Telegram, the United States declares war on Germany.

May - French army units mutiny during the unsuccessful Nivelle Offensive, refusing to attack German positions.

July - The Battle of Passchendaele (Third Battle of Ypres) begins on the 31st; it will drag on into November, with heavy casualties on both sides.

November - The Battle of Caporetto, also called the Twelfth Battle of the Isonzo, ends with the Italian army in tatters. In Russia, the radical Bolsheviks overthrow the Provisional Government; within a month, the Bolsheviks have signed an armistice with the Central Powers.

1918

March - Russia officially surrenders in the Treaty of Brest-Litovsk (March 3). Germany begins a series of offensives on the Western Front.

July - American and French forces counterattack the Germans along the Marne.

September - The Allied "grand offensive" on the Western Front begins on Sept. 26 with the American-led Meuse-Argonne Offensive. Bulgaria signs an armistice.

October - Allied forces overwhelm the Hindenburg Line. The Ottoman Empire signs an armistice on the 30th.

November - Austria-Hungary signs an armistice (Nov. 3). Kaiser Wilhelm abdicates. The fighting in World War I ends on Nov. 11, when Germany signs an armistice.

1919

On June 28, the Treaty of Versailles is signed.

CHAPTER NOTES

p. 7:   "You will be home . . ." Barbara W. Tuchman, *The Guns of August* (New York: Ballantine Books, 1994), p. 119.

p. 7:   "We none of us . . ." Philipp Witkop, *German Students' War Letters* (Philadelphia: University of Pennsylvania Press, 2013), pp. 2–3.

p. 8:   "parades in the street . . ." Stefan Zweig, *The World of Yesterday: An Autobiography* (Lincoln: University of Nebraska Press, 1964), p. 223.

p. 11:   "All sides are preparing . . ." David Fromkin, *Europe's Last Summer: Who Started the Great War in 1914?* (New York: Alfred A. Knopf, 2004), p. 31.

p. 13:   "every cause for war . . ." Ibid., p. 218.

p. 18:   "We must allow the enemy . . ." John Keegan, *The First World War* (New York: Vintage Books, 2000), p. 101.

p. 20:   "We shall be crushed . . ." Michael S. Neiberg, *Fighting the Great War: A Global History* (Cambridge, MA: Harvard University Press, 2005), p. 32.

p. 29:   "to drowning only . . ." Gilbert King, "Fritz Haber's Experiments in Life and Death," Smithsonian.com, June 6, 2012. http://www.smithsonianmag.com/history/fritz-habers-experiments-in-life-and-death-114161301/?no-ist

p. 35:   "bleeding white . . ." Robert T. Foley, *German Strategy and the Path to Verdun: Erich von Falkenhayn and the Development of Attrition, 1870–1916* (Cambridge, UK: Cambridge University Press, 2005), p. 197.

p. 37:   "You will find the Germans . . ." G. J. Meyer, *A World Undone: The Story of the Great War, 1914 to 1918* (New York: Bantam Dell, 2007), p. 438.

p. 40:   "Our thoughts are chiefly . . ." Evelyn Mary Stapleton-Bretherton Blücher von Wahlstatt, *An English Wife in Berlin: A Private Memoir of Events, Politics, and Daily Life Throughout the War and the Social Revolution of 1918* (New York: E. P. Dutton & Co., 1920), pp. 158–59.

p. 42:   "This war could not . . ." Elizabeth Frost-Knappman and Kathryn Cullen-DuPont, *Women's Suffrage in America* (New York: Infobase Publishing, 2009), p. 424.

p. 45:   "The hour of sacrifice . . ." John Lichfield, "A History of the First World War in 100 Moments: The Nivelle Offensive—When the

Lambs Refused to March to the Slaughter," *The Independent*, June 8, 2014. http://www.independent.co.uk/news/world/world-history/history-of-the-first-world-war-in-100-moments/a-history-of-the-first-world-war-in-100-moments-the-nivelle-offensive--when-the-lambs-refused-to-march-to-the-slaughter-9509819.html

p. 45:   "heard nothing but . . ." Ibid.

p. 51:   "the blackest day . . ." Williamson Murray, *Military Adaptation in War: With Fear of Change* (Cambridge, UK: Cambridge University Press, 2011), p. 116.

p. 53:   "Every soldier who fights . . ." Herbert George Wells, *The War That Will End War* (New York: Duffield & Co., 1914), p. 14.

.

FURTHER READING

Barber, Nicola. *World War I*. Mankato, MN: Heinemann-Raintree, 2012.

Clark, Christopher. *The Sleepwalkers: How Europe Went to War in 1914*. London: Allen Lane, 2012.

Hochschild, Adam. *To End All Wars: A Story of Loyalty and Rebellion, 1914–1918*. New York: Houghton Mifflin Harcourt, 2011.

Philpott, William. *War of Attrition: Fighting the First World War*. New York: The Overlook Press, 2014.

Rasmussen, R. Kent. *World War I for Kids: A History with 21 Activities*. Chicago: Chicago Review Press, 2014.

Storey, Neil R., and Molly Housego. *Women in the First World War*. Oxford, UK: Osprey Publishing, Ltd., 2010.

INTERNET RESOURCES

http://www.pbs.org/greatwar/

> The companion website to the PBS documentary *The Great War and the Making of the 20th Century.*

http://www.history.army.mil/books/AMH-V2/PDF/ Chapter01.pdf

> An overview of the U.S. Army during World War I.

http://www.bbc.com/ww1/

> The British Broadcasting Corporation's World War I site offers video reports, podcasts, archival photos and film, analysis by historians, and much more.

Publisher's Note: The websites listed on this page were active at the time of publication. The publisher is not responsible for websites that have changed their address or discontinued operation since the date of publication. The publisher reviews and updates the websites each time the book is reprinted.

INDEX

Numbers in ***bold italics*** refer to captions.

SERIES GLOSSARY

blockade—an effort to cut off supplies, war material, or communications in a particular area, by force or the threat of force.

guerrilla warfare—a type of warfare in which a small group of combatants, such as armed civilians, use hit-and-run tactics to fight a larger and less mobile traditional army. The purpose is to weaken an enemy's strength through small skirmishes, rather than fighting pitched battles where the guerrillas would be at a disadvantage.

intelligence—the analysis of information collected from various sources in order to provide guidance and direction to military commanders.

logistics—the planning and execution of movements by military forces, and the supply of those forces.

salient—a pocket or bulge in a fortified line or battle line that projects into enemy territory.

siege—a military blockade of a city or fortress, with the intent of conquering it at a later stage.

tactics—the science and art of organizing a military force, and the techniques for using military units and their weapons to defeat an enemy in battle.